Martyn Crucefix

Hurt

ENITHARMON PRESS

First published in 2010
by Enitharmon Press
26B Caversham Road
London NW5 2DU

www.enitharmon.co.uk

Distributed in the UK by
Central Books
99 Wallis Road
London E9 5LN

Distributed in the USA and Canada
by Dufour Editions Inc.
PO Box 7, Chester Springs
PA 19425, USA

ISBN: 978-1-904634-97-3

Enitharmon Press gratefully acknowledges the
financial support of Arts Council England.

British Library Cataloguing-in-Publication Data.
A catalogue record for this book is available
from the British Library.

Designed in Albertina by Libanus Press

Printed and bound in Great Britain by
CPI Antony Rowe, Chippenham and Eastbourne

Hurt

for Margaret and Raymond
who loved the island

ACKNOWLEDGEMENTS

My thanks to those who have been kind enough to comment on this book in its making, particularly Andrew Brenner, Neil Curry, Valerie Jack, Mario Petrucci, James Wykes.

'More than it comes to' owes a lot to Walt Whitman's *Memoranda during the War* and his letters so that parts of my poem might be considered 'found'. 'Growth of a poet's mind' draws details from *Young Stalin*, Simon Sebag Montefiore (Weidenfeld & Nicolson, 2007).

Some of these poems, or earlier versions of them, have appeared in: *Magma, Acumen, www.bowwowshop.org.uk, The Cortland Review* (USA), *The Frogmore Papers, Iota, The London Magazine, Long Poem Magazine, Poetry London, The Rialto, Scintilla, Shearsman, The Spectator, Staple, nthposition.com.*

'Invocation' - under the title 'Chasing the nightjar' - was a prizewinner in the Troubadour Poetry Prize 2007. 'A truck called Perseverance' was short-listed in the Iota International Poetry Competition, 2009.

Sie aber sind ja
unser winterwähriges Laub, unser dunkeles Sinngrün,
eine der Zeiten des heimlichen Jahres—, nicht nur
Zeit — sind Stelle, Siedelung, Lager, Boden, Wohnort.

Yet they are our winter leaves, our dark evergreen,
one season of our secret year – not only a season,
but a site, settlement, camp, soil and resting place.

Rilke, *Duino Elegies*, 10

CONTENTS

III Riders on the storm

I
At the cross-hairs

INVOCATION

These days they say she's sometimes mistaken
for the revving of a little petrol engine –

her propulsive *churr-churring* lost in the dark.
But age-old tricks can still be made to work.

Launch a white handkerchief into the air
and – if you are lucky – she's gliding there,

attracted to you like a catch in the throat,
summoned by signs of life – the hot, the salt

of sudden tears you'd rather were hidden,
making your nose run like a child's again.

Or she's drawn to the blood-spill of hurt
that opens flesh and bone. Or she will start

from the dusty roof-space above the bed,
find you wiping love from between your legs.

The white flag of individual weakness
is what serves always to conjure her best

as when old habits, uncertain eyes give out,
when it's dark wherever they put the light,

she comes then – I think – and this time stays,
cover him, cover him, cover his face.

WATER-LILY

I

Mysterious - priapic - in her slow ascent
through olive-green, cloudy, particulate water.

Scarcely predicted, but looked-for for days,
her dark bomb rising, an old balancing act

on a turgid stalk. Upped in blind pursuit,
her slow-motion chasing out-riding scouts:

that series of pan-flat, broadening leaves
that wince red to racing green at the strain

of powering out of the pond's darkest places.
Imagined only by those who stoop low enough,

I see the crud, skeletal leaves, the sink away
to another dimension. Here at last she comes,

tracked close at four, three, two inches shy
of this world, seldom seen broaching herself

in the sun-warm air, the blue-lit afternoon.
In that instant becomes her own subject saying:

II

me, talk about me, about my tear-drop shape,
my split heart opening to kissable pink. Look!

Little raptor head! My dense-packed bud!
My elegant lack of interest in what lies ahead.

Out of this darkness, I leap to such climax,
to this ball-gown flounce I know is enough.

Not this distraught look, your agitated air.
Your stink. Your nice understanding! Talk!

Not your species' love of persecution –
no better reason than you mislike a face!

Not promises, cross-tongued, double-crossed,
all weakness, petty, knife-edged, taint.

Look how I rise – my focus, my intensity!
I am my own device. Then damn what's behind.

I give nothing of myself. All I want is free.
Shake off this idiocy! Take a look at me!

III

You stoop to find she cannot be still for long:
her surface beauty equivalent to being young.

You see the crud, skeletal leaves, the sink back,
say you've no reply to what she just said

since you carry such freight, so much baggage,
the worst and best of it your love of language.

Waiting like a spider at the cross-hairs
of words and things, you screw up in a moment,

lose it from paying too little attention,
from remaining shut tight in flesh and bone,

your eyes diminished with other men's dreams,
trying ideas, emotions like cast-off clothes.

You know little of yourself, less of others
but if once in a while the cross-hairs align,

straight, true, you say this, this is mine.
The report echoes long after the lily survives.

WHILE THERE IS WAR
Table and Chair by Peter Coker

This must be the filthy sink.
This beige-brown door leading off
to a brown-beige place . . .
A dirt-grey floor promises
at first sight only dull support.
A table and a chair of wood:
something like deal and language
such as *scrubbed* and *plain*
will prove quite good enough.

Yet the boy is a bright one.
You only have to look in his eye.
At the table's grain-marked end,
muscular cooking-apples,
a soup bowl, a glass bottle
shows the blinding white of milk,
a colander set to do service,
a fork lies at the ready.

These few shell-like objects
scattered under the boy's gaze
might be oysters. Perhaps nuts.
A word like *beechmast*
would report them well enough.
And the red splash that seizes
the eye of every on-looker –
that must be considered last.

It's a flayed death's head
someone has laid on a newspaper
to look like ketchup and chips:
in fact, it's the head of a sheep.

Such items fill the table-top.
But the boy does not climb to it.
He does not clamber down and away.
Despite everything, the boy
seems prepared to stand there
counting.

BEYOND THE BEE FARM
for Jess and Sophia

The queen's head daubed
for ease of handling.
The ventilator gang set,
wing-beats revving
to cool the teeming hive
where every worker
appears busy – unlike you,
on the hillside later.

A lone speck buzzing
tight sabre-curving strokes
about the blonde head
of the child that walks
beside me – your wings
accelerating, a blur
of bee-malice, razor-edged,
now buried in her hair.

I watch this from above,
see you wrestling rope.
I nudge, disentangle.
It's you I try to help
but some fogged confusion,
stray puff of breeze,
flicks you sideways –
her sister's cardigan sleeve

where, glossy abdomen
curving, you thrust down
through gaping sink-holes
of knitted honeycomb.
My fingers bully now,

pushing, shoving you,
no longer certain
who needs to be rescued.

You streak past my eye
to floppy folds of hair,
a choleric head-noise,
a thrill in my ear –
tiny reflex stinger
finds my scalp, goes in.
Next morning, sitting out
as other bees skim

from bloom to sweet bloom
(oh, my honey-pie!)
as if no hurt in the world,
as if we both survived.
I saw the cap and spike,
the tiny black thorn
like a kaiser's helmet
as it was withdrawn

delicately from my head
as your wrecked self
never made the burrow
I knew nothing of . . .
My head healed quickly.
Your pain was shorter.
Name me the gods who
make us hurt each other.

STAG BEETLE

More than an hour ago
you gave up the task,
blaming bad-egg odours
sniffed in these joints.
In such heat, already
the tight-packed innards
beginning to shrivel.
Now disentangling again
these extraordinary legs
with the nib of a pen
you unpack sheathed uppers
and balletic elbows,
these rough serrations
beyond spindly wrists,
my six feet like clamps
like a chameleon's . . .
What you think could be
ball-and-socket joints
abut the shell that gleams
less ebony in this light
that leaves you floundering.
What you want to know
is how it feels locked
in insensitive plate
with the world of signals
intrusive only from
a few live ends. You try
to imagine how it must be
to live within edges
toothed and raw, a pack
of saws ripped from some
black hole in creation.
You tease antlers apart

try to peer at what lies
beneath my pitch-black
forehead, but only find
a nest of feelers,
each furred and rooted
too deeply to betray
even a glimmer of purpose.
In the palm of your hand
I lie, seeming alien,
but you have forgotten
mysteries you pursue
at night without a word
to where she sleeps
beside you – or to others
who raised you, walking
far more stiff-legged
and beetle-like now –
or children rising tall
on the terrace outside,
excited at what you see
as an unremarkable
view of the hills that
for them is trembling
on the brink of singing,
an excitable world
to which you bring only
puzzlement or derision.
O yes I am the stag
of your age and occlusion.
You must fight me now.
I am not yet dead.

CELL

Word is they gather
round tiny glasses
of sweetened coffee.
Organise mostly
in one another's
rooms: photocopies,
chanting, precious books.
Yet their final goal
still remains obscure,
though we understand
these groups: their systems
of mutual support,
reverence for age,
even youngsters praised.
Transcripts of meetings
show therapeutic
elements: more art
than *realpolitik* –
vague and alarming.
Silence. Spoken words.
No suspicious files,
no guns, explosives.
Long experience
shows something alive,
but how to be sure
where this might lead them.
We trace their retreat
far beyond our reach
into mundane lives,
but cannot record
what secret they keep.
When they are ready,
they'll speak as one.
That day they're done.

GROWTH OF A POET'S MIND

1. Start

The seventeen-year-old
with the burning eyes, the swept-back
slick of black hair
wants to be a priest.

Instead he takes
a sheaf of close-written papers
to Chavchavadze's office,
its chaos of scripts and books,
something unfinished
rolled through the typewriter:

all this tilting as the youth
stands radiant with sex
as much as religion,
the cobbler's son beaten
at home to a brawler on the street.

He knows the seminary is better than
all this, demands as much
of words to which he aspires,
being handsome and pock-marked.

With one strong arm, one withered,
he walks out less conscious
of his two webbed feet now,
ears ringing with official praise.

2. Work

This one addressed to
the chilly tireless moon, an outcast
in a world of ice

and god's providence, of many things
remote and distantly glorious.

These becoming his task masters:
marshalled into the work
in which even an oppressed man
before he cries out for food
strives again to reach the pure mountain.

Or this one – of a prophet
poisoned by his own people.
Or this, concerning wisdom,
with a harp to inspire,

an armed figure to frighten,
dreaming of the past
and telling his children's children

how he'd strip his vest,
thrust his chest towards the moon,
without waiting
compose the moon's response.

3. Enthusiast

A glacier on the streets of Tiflis
they called him – a hoodlum
but the pearl of his verses
was more than proof enough
for me on meeting him once again.

It was at the Narikala café
where I'd lunch alternate days,
three hundred yards from the Bank.

I understood his purpose
when I began to recite those poems:
the kind of clarity and conviction
that cuts like a knife.

Until I had the information –
the arrival by stagecoach
of a million roubles and nothing
I might ever regret
though it's been said I set him on
to pollution by others . . .

The money was well-spent
though like shards of a blown safe maybe
forty bodies littered the street.

4. Art

In this country, poetry is valued highly:
they may kill you for it
being a question of style.

So it's important you do your best
to compose it as the man would want it.
The youth grown into his tyranny.

He prefers abstraction in language:
isolate but preserve.
Prefers to indulge in mockery now
of the truly gifted,
though walking blind all the while

to the ubiquity of error,
how it's woven into being 'human'.

We all know someone
who has heard him complain
how words wanted too much attention –
or how he grows effusive

about patience, saying,
I had little such patience
since I was – I was quicksilver he says
seeing before him
the flick of a street blade.

DIARY OF ONE WHO DISAPPEARED
Janacek JW 5/12

This piece for solo voice
and piano: both have turned
their backs to the window
I unlocked earlier
to let a cool breeze in
for this young audience
as they follow the music
up and down. The window
opens onto an alley
that travels a few yards
to a murmur of traffic
on Brent Street. Some of us
(the least attentive)
catch sight of shoppers
strolling past or pick out
scraps of passing talk
till a grey, untidy head
comes to a halt outside.
Thin-lipped, she blankly
stares at neither singer
nor seated pianist . . .
Nor does she fix her gaze
on faces around the room.
Outside, a breath of wind
stirs, then slips across
the sill to lift a sheet
of music from its stand.
Just in time, the singer's
quick professional hand
sets it back in place.
And still, her steady head
in silence is inclined

to the kind of pleasures
sad music affords. Then
'Bravo!' in a hoarse,
thick accent she calls,
as soon sinks from sight,
reappears – her raised hand
crossing the window-sill –
she introduces a yellow
flower she has plucked
from the foot of the wall.
She calls again "Bravo!"
and my eyes are shut
to see desolate streets,
neighbourhoods failed,
find kicked-in doorways
left open to the rain,
track her disappeared
into camps and ditches,
the lucky scattering
where their journey slows
to this pedal-note of
idling cars, these brown,
pallid and olive faces,
this sunlit afternoon
in this English town,
these peremptory gifts
from one already gone.

CASIDA OF THE WEEPING
from Lorca

I have closed off my balcony
because I do not want to hear the weeping;
yet from behind grey walls
nothing else can be heard but the weeping.

There are so few angels that sing,
there are so few dogs that bark,
a thousand violins sit in the palm of my hand.

But the weeping is an enormous dog,
the weeping is an enormous angel,
the weeping is an enormous violin,
the tears stifle the wind,
and nothing else can be heard but the weeping.

MORE THAN IT COMES TO

seven poems from the American War

I. I pick'd up my pen

I pick'd up my pen & wrote my mother,
That I knew how she suffered with the passing of these days,
That all she might cling to since George's last was my news.
That I had my pocket picked changing cars at Philadelphia,
That I landed here without a dime, coming in a jam and hurry.
Yet I wrote her my particular difficulties were but trifles,
In contrast to those moments in Brooklyn that still repeat themselves:
Our knowledge that George's whereabouts were no longer known,
And the possibility that he was no more,
And in those moments nothing to stop our livid imagining of war,
As we pursue it along the banks of the Rappahannock.

I wrote her how our lively imaginings are hourly surpassed.
Since my arriving opposite Fredericksburgh the 19th,
Even my concern to find our own flesh and blood has been surpassed.
I saw the Lacy house, a brick mansion of the long-gone days,
I saw a tree within 10 yards of the front of the house,
And at the foot of the tree a heap of amputated legs & arms & hands.
I saw bodies lying near, each cover'd with its own woolen blanket,
I saw fresh graves in the door-yard,
The names on pieces of barrel-staves or scratched on broken boards.
I wrote what I saw which is something not seen in Brooklyn.
It is what men try to keep close for fear of a mother's reply,
For fear of a strident reply spoken by the mothers of Americans.
Yet if we cannot feel as we must, what is it we are come to,
Fighting here on the sandy banks of the Rappahannock?

So I pick'd up my pen & addressed all American mothers,
That this land may as well lie on the farthest side of the earth.
That I have walked well-shod round Falmouth and Rappahannock,

That the length of each hour is imbu'd with a knowledge:
Of how the earth has never been so shaken by artificial means,
That the air has never reverberated as on that wintry daybreak,
In an instant the big and little thunderers in chorus began to roar.
I am witness to their progeny in Camp, Brigade and Division Hospitals,
Where many die each day, though our George, as I found him,
Was yet safe and well, and was in health, with a good appetite,
Though he was more wearied and homesick than he allowed,
Where we sat quiet on the banks of the Rappahannock.

II. The White House

Tonight, I walk out to take a look at the President's House.
Tonight, the white portico, the brilliant gas-light shining,
The palace-like pediment, the tall round columns, spotless as snow.
Tonight, a tender and soft moonlight flooding the pale marble,
A light that gives rise to peculiar & faint & languishing shades,
That are not shadows, for no such thing as shadow resides at this address.

On this night, a soft transparent haze under the thin moon-lace,
Where it falls amongst the bright and plentiful clusters of gas-lights,
That have been set at intervals around the façade & the columns.
Tonight, I see everything white, a marbly pure white and dazzling,
And even more so, the softest white of the White House of future poems,
And of dramas and dreams here, under the high, the copious moon.

Tonight, the pure and gorgeous front in trees under the night-lights,
The leafless silence and the trunks and myriad angles of branches.
Tonight, I see a White House of the land, a White House of the night,
And of beauty and of silence and sentries at the tall gate,
Sentries pacing in their blue overcoats, stopping me not at all,
But eyeing with their sharp sentries' eyes whichever way I go.

III. I dream'd a stockade

I dream'd a stockade fallen into decay, a time when the war was done.
Long years in the future, I dream'd our American land secure,
But on waking the need still to sing a million pains & the many dead:
Of the soldier wounded at Fredericksberg,
Who lay the succeeding two days and nights helpless on the field;
Of another brave soldier who bore it well,
Having loose splinters of bone taken from the neighbourhood of a wound;
Of the nurse in Ward Seventeen who relieved a dying soldier,
Of the cloth she held carefully to his mouth as he coughed up blood;
Of the handsome New Yorker shot through the bladder,
The shot hitting him in the front of the belly and coming out back,
Of the water that came from the wound and other disagreeable
        circumstances;
Of another young man who was wounded before Atlanta,
This man was a rebel and mortally wounded in the top of his head,
His heel scraping the ground digging a hole enough for two knapsacks;
Of this being repeated at Bull Run, at Chancellorsville,
At Columbia, Tennessee, and Susquehannah, the dead and wounded,
Up from Charleston, Savannah, up from the battlefields of the South,
Virginia, the Peninsula, Malvern Hill and Fair Oaks,
Chickahominy, Antietam Bridge, the ravines of Manassas,
The Mississippi freshets, Gettysburgh & Vicksburg & Petersburgh.
Still unfinish'd, my song of the million pains & so many dead:
Of the two officers, feet pinn'd to the ground by bayonets,
Of sharp blades stuck through them, they receiv'd twenty thrusts.
Of the seventeen captured, encompass'd, humiliated and finally shot;
Of typhoid fever and camp fevers generally,
Of catarrhal affections and bronchitis, diarrhoea, rheumatism,
        pneumonia,
Of the wolf's and lion's lapping thirst for blood,
Of the light of burning farms,
Of the light of burning homes and towns,
Of the sudden light of explosions,
And in the human heart on every side, the worsening black embers I sing,

And dream still of a stockade grown upon by the creeping grasses,
So that only one season more may obliterate it completely,
The creeping grasses only now rolling across the dead line,
Of the line over which so many brave soldiers from all sides pass'd,
And many pass'd to be effac'd with the years,
If not from my heart, not from my memory, not from my song.

IV. I staid a long time to-night

I staid a long time to-night at his difficult bed-side.
It was a young Baltimorean, grown to the age of nineteen.
He had seen so much and yet had slept such a very little,
His right leg amputated an hour since, he was feeble,
So he slept hardly at all, the morphine costing more than it comes to.

And this is what I must do, I sit still while he holds my hand,
And he puts it to his face most affectionately.
And this young, handsome, tanned Baltimorean spoke to me:
'My dear friend, I am certain you do not know who I am,
Although your sitting here so quietly and so patiently,
It means much, yet you must understand who it is you help,
Since what I stand for & fight for I know you believe to be wrong'.

I staid a long time at the bed-side of the young Baltimorean.
I staid certainly because death had mark'd him and he was quite alone.
I might say I loved him, sometimes kiss'd him and he did me.
And of his age was his brother, a brave and religious man,
His brother and officer of rank, a man I sat beside in a close,
        adjoining ward.

And I staid because in the same battle they were wounded alike,
The one strong Unionist, the other Secesh, and each fought well,
Each for their respective sides, brave & obedient & mark'd for the end.
Now they lay close, following the separation of many years,
Of their strongly held beliefs, the separations these had imposed on them,
And both fought well and each died in his particular cause.

V. The President

The President pass'd by where I stood & I could see him well.
I saw he was very plain and substantial,
And when people speak of him they speak in hushed tones.
They say he is riding from Vermont Avenue to Pennsylvania Avenue.
They say his party is not one to make a great show in uniforms or horses.
They say his look is of a good man (and I believe there is much in looks).

Nor can I forget the first time I set undimm'd eyes upon him:
A man whose stove-pipe hat was pushed back on his dark head,
A man possessed of very little popularity in the city of New York.
A man not concerned to be shown the usual demonstrations of that city,
The deafening tumults of welcome not to be trusted,
The thunder-shout of the pack'd myriads along the line of Broadway.

The President pass'd by where I stood,
And I saw a man able to face for over a minute a vast & silent crowd,
A man slowly and good-humouredly able to scan their true appearance.
A man seemingly unaware of so many eyes upon him.
I saw a man contained in himself, I believe I saw a man we might trust.

VI. To the Mother of one fallen

This is not the page you would have of me,
And yet I must write, being a friend who sat at his deathbed.
And I can tell you he was wounded very badly in the left leg,
And he was sent up to Washington, to the Armoury Square hospital,
And his leg was amputated a little above the knee.
There I witness'd the operation by a surgeon whose name is Bliss,
And the doctor advis'd there was a deal of bad matter in the wound,
And for a time your son was doing well.

Hence I took it upon myself to visit very frequently,
And I believe he was fond of having me sit quietly & close.
But in time your son's case grew critical with fevers & cold spells,
And in the last week of April he was flighty much of the time.

I have seen many, so I know your son's was a good death.
The cause of it was pyaemia, the absorption of bad matter,
That is taken into the system rather than given proper discharge.
He liked to put out an arm and lay his hand on my knee.
Near the end, he was strange & restless in the night particularly,
And he often fancied himself with his regiment,
And his speech was of hurt feeling, of how he had suffered blame.
His commanding officer blamed him for something he had not done,
And he was entirely innocent of this crime I am sure.

And then he would fancy himself talking again,
As it seem'd to children, or such like, his relatives, I suppos'd.
And he would talk with them a long while.
And though he was far out of his head for much of this time,
Not one bad word or bad idea did I hear escape him,
So though I knew little of his past life I felt it must have been good.
And afterwards I thought some word worth the while,
Even from a stranger, even one who was with him to the last,
For as soon as I saw him I loved your son, this young man,
Though I only saw him immediately to lose him again.

VII. To his own Mother

Little California is playing here about me as I settle to write.
She has been playing half an hour, not suspecting what I am at.
Line on line, this is something I send to the grieving,
To those with you who have not the remotest idea what I have seen,
Nor what has passed before me in the hospitals,
What passes on the fields, in the soldiers' shebang enclosures of bushes.

My spirits tire of months spent wrestling with this, dear mother,
As if my mind must be always standing on the tip of its toes,
Or else be struck down, or turn off to one side, or shut these eyes,
Which is only then to comprehend the fires that light such dark.
They are each one yours and Han's and George's and Andrew's,

They are yours and Jeff's and his little Manahatta's too.
And in your eyes shut time, mother, is not one burning light a boy's,
Your American boy, your boy first, your son, a boy still?

I have to tell you Burnside's army passed through here yesterday.
And all of those brave men, they also are all boys.
I saw their naked limbs through the scurf of well-worn clothes,
I saw their thin bundles and knapsacks, the clatter of tin cups.
Some had frying pans strapt over their backs, all dirty & sweaty.
There seemed nothing neat about them but their muskets.
Such flesh as they had, I thought it glowed through their clothes,
And I had a vision in which for some time I saw Rebel armies too,
And each walking the same path beside our beautiful Potomac.

It is true, of course, that I am not well these days.
It is most likely hospital poison has penetrated my system.
But do not think of me this way, do not see your boy this way,
Remember me as I was and must surely be again.
See my beard and neck grown woollier, fleecier, whiteyer than ever,
See me weighing fully 220 pounds avoirdupois,
See my trouser-tops tuck'd into black morocco boots,
See me going about well-shod and -legged to face the deep Virginian muds,
And oh! about these majestic brows I will clap a hat,
My well-brimmed felt hat with the black and gold cord with acorns,
And see guards in blue coats admire me as I pass and sometimes salute,
Dress'd so, your boy in his black hat and his black boots, I pass.

II
Essays in island logic

'Same sea, same dangers waiting for him
As though he had got nowhere but older'

W. S. Merwin – 'Odysseus'

HE CONSIDERS THE PASSAGE OF TIME

old man walking retirement

up the hillside below the pine belts
past centuries-old spilled

sarcophagi looking
to recover one particular grave *stele* —
this

sure as he can be
this one under a triangular pediment
the young man leaning back in bas relief

such a contemporary slouch
legs crossed at the ankles hips thrust out
in contemplation

a warrior's helmet held at arm's length
its long plume

like a lion's tail
seeming about to respond to his ambitious

nature his searching
out the end of all complexity —

sees now the boy's had his forehead
chipped off
the kid is brainless and beautiful

about second century BC
marking the grave of a dead warrior

an old man all but forgotten
after dusk

walking retirement down the dark hillside
bringing it to the surf's edge now

like a child

HE HAS TO MAKE HIS OWN BED

loves this steady climb
even to find she's stripped it to launder

has to pull clean from the creaking basket
launch sheets across it
fisting pillows into pillowcase mouths

all the time believing he must
but tonight finding it
difficult to resist the vanished past —

so many men of the island
built bedrooms about olive trees

gnarled trunks trimmed until smooth
an adze steady in hand

only pausing to run a finger
up the solid bed-post then falling to
eager and passionate

pushing on to confirm
the firm centre
the writhe and rhythm of generation —

absurd and primitive
as deep purple dye inlaid with silver
and gold

yet each achieved a royal bed of sorts
roots at their furthest reaches

growing intimate with roots of neighbours'

straining olives he feels now

too queasy a thought
one hand heavy on the banister's climb

to uneventful bed

HIS SON WAKES AND WANDERS ROUND THE HOUSE

stirring in the small of night

the boy raises himself to a gluey throat
fattened lips

feels his way
downstairs to the unlit kitchen

to be surprised by the winking of lights
like campfire signs
wasteful stand-bys burning

on the distant hillside
of radio microwave fridge oven —

leans into polished taps
knocks back glass after re-hydrating glass

dregs of last night's beer
incline him to hear the muttering of troops

on the dark flanks of hills

the clank of billies scouring of blade edges
a vastness of purpose
drawing up the life he never possessed —

knows he would have been astute
clear-headed then
consulted through the terrific nights

by faithful generals
who'd hymn his black ferocity

his desire for the acid tests of dawn
that will never come
but the obscurities of blame

upstairs his father singing in his sheets
dull as new-born

HIS WIFE IS RESTLESS IN HER SLEEP

a girl once more shepherding the flock
of twenty geese

like pets she lords it over them
a pack of baying dogs

showing pale against dark volcanic soil
waddling from the round pond

on her father's farm
crowding to eat the grain she lends them

till eagle cruelty with steely talons
sweeps out of a sky
apparently twenty years deep —

feathers
explosive as when white cherry blossom
is ripped by the wind

a blur of wing white/black failing

she screams wrestling to beat
the bird off in vain
her flock a shredded bloodied mattress —

imperious eagle on the roof-tree

tilting its eye to ocean distance
into blue ocean
it's me your husband come to set you free

her sphere of influence diminished
twenty-fold

but continues to be grateful
touching heaviness in her right breast
cannot recall

how many times she has dreamed this

HIS SON'S DREAM IS OF A NEW BEGINNING

it blows like Mount St Helens

some plantation farmer
offering three women he knows
as unwilling sacrifice

to appease what he seriously calls
the volcanic gods
but the DJ declines

there are too few people laughing
too many climbing into the front of trucks —

all lights and reasonable instruments
melted in the first blast

all wax-hanging globules of plastic
a new native art

ripening towards exploitation
as individuals begin to paint
volcanic ash in albumen

as if that mix might
usher in secure economic governance
a bright-lit future —

still others regardless have begun
to reconfigure Year Zero
till no-one confesses suffering troubled

sleep sense of impotence
strange unfixable guilts resistant

even to waking
as if what just hurtled with such clarity
through a young man's head

might never happen

HE CONSIDERS THE PROCESS OF HISTORY

from his eyrie starts
awake to the increasing white cliffs
of tourist palaces

their long blue necklaces of pools
lessons in history in his morning glimpse
of black-rock coastline dragging itself

from the glittering ocean off-comers
come for —

a graph line of island population
first registering in rock-pool shallows

gathering to a barely visible invasion
of black-grit beaches

sudden
vertical lurching up the volcanic cliff-face

from which all the insular myths
have flowed —

the heroic defence of a once-chosen race
proud statues
of outstanding individualists

a glorious empire of ruins
and footholds explosive progress of suitors
and singles

sharks and shysters
piling their millions into breezeblock
apartments

lamps and leatherwear
cheques and beer and bermudas dropped

at twinkling nightfall
finding their way to washed-up dawn

HIS WIFE PASSES THE HARBOUR CLUB

after nature's nine-month stretch
of body-heat sculling yes

tradition must bring children
to land via water

with it's easier birth
to match the significance of the sea
to the island

where pools feature
at all important transitions —

birthdays are fluid
mid-seasons marked by dousing
splashy races the pubertal dive

the marital ducking
and death she thought this morning
stepping from the shower

a solemn embarkation
our sons and daughters schooled in scuba
snorkel crawl back 'fly —

but tradition comes under threat
like the snagged marlin
their reflex to rebel

to wrestle the line unreeling
to this troubled longing for dust this
desire for flight

even as their elders coerce them
into glittering water

they cry out to be wearing goggles
they look lost nervous angry

out of place

HE CONSIDERS IMPROVEMENTS ON THE ISLAND

hand-in-glove with mainland government
they automatise

the lighthouse
that has long set its foot
in basalt veins under Black Point

convert the lighthouse-keeper's rooms
to holiday lets
as if we did not have enough —

till the last keeper
is drunk all day on the marina wall

has visions
grows full of omens

the squabbling children
pelt him with crab shells and fish ends

loitering for hours after nightfall
his quiet staring
into the rhythm of his usurped home —

its appointment
flawless now the machinery pulses
and the human plays dumb

as dough-bodied hermits
revert to submergence and silence
as he is driven

to and fro by the tide
striking out for borrowed shells

every gesture becoming more imprecise
every gesture
becoming obscured by the night

the ghostly
tongue-tied disenfranchised soul

HIS SON REHEARSES ONE OF THEIR MANY ARGUMENTS

petals explodes the angry young man
stammering oath on oath

at what his own feet trample on
scarcely glorified sea-bed

nothing more than rock and sand
in the cold deeps

where light does not come
where life
is an afterthought if it's anything at all —

such noisy convictions
that even earth's imprisoned and incapable
it cannot choose

but rather balloons out at random
rupture he cries
about which old men know fucking plenty

innards extruded molten rock
earth of course in search of definition
gas and fire

mixed with the freeze of water
is all —

over and over this same mistake
this same spill spew going solid to pile
a homeland

its unforgiving soil
this scurf of life that sprawls across it

says his father
I know what you say but try to explain

purple petals
on my doorstep all summer long

HIS WIFE WATCHES A FRAGMENT OF ROCK

where her husband
rakes black leaves from the blue water
she watches them ruddy their faces

off-comers holding their breath behind
the Paradise Hotel

words like *appointment*
second quarter cumulative results
becoming a strange language to them —

their longest meeting poolside at noon
where dolphin-like

they go ducking for silly-coloured stones
the stubbled father
resting one on his belly

floating
as youngsters splash to plunder it
folding up around the black

micro-aerated chunk of volcanic clinker
picked from the wall —

the eye of a shark
once punched well past the cruising height
of in-coming white jets

extruded at such extravagant pressures
superheated shot past

self-determination
the long wait paying off now time settles
to slower rhythms

it sidles
down through clear blue water

HIS SON EARNS A LIVING

loves them to pursue the nothings
they gather on the quay-side in search of

fleeces them at the marina
framed photos at the point of embarkation
all shades and absurd hats

not enough sun-screen
their spoilt children stepping off
into space —

onto the paint-blistered deck of his father's
old cruiser

where they flog out over the white-tops
to tuna and dolphin

see bow-racing flashes of rubberised skin
like grey inner-tubes

he'd drown as a boy on the look-out
for quivering silver —

he sees the vessel's white returning prow
has time for a couple more

is never tempted
since no more than a summer month of this
is enough to despise their hankering

their wistful looking-out-to-sea look
even as grinning strings
of harbour lights blink on heavenly

as they say to him always
in the same sequence he finds himself
counting

pockets full of coin

HE CONSIDERS THE CREATURES OF THE ISLAND

nothing like the wagtail
stooping from the jacaranda to the street
barely a claw-print to be traced

nor like lizards
slipped thin as dusty wire

from beneath the bushes
of the Harbour Swimming Club
licking drops of spilt ice-cream

not the smallest part
of the many forces of erosion —

by no means does he conceive of himself
as a flock of clumsy pigeon

with their mocking wing-flap plaudits
pecking at random the job undone

not even grey mullet
at their weaving under his narrowed eye
beneath the wall of the marina

kilos of silty fish-muscle
scribbling a slippery chaos —

but he grows warmer
to think of the manners of the shark

its curiosity
in being driven to every scrap
of its devouring

as if in praise
as if being drawn into the circle
of strange new appetites

and one of these this way of seeing
everything
mixed undressed all one

HIS WIFE SHOPS FOR THE EVENING MEAL

she admires them

bringing their brisk cool-weather business
nous with them

they take up struggling corner shops
begin to flourish
since who does not need fruit a sweet-burst

cigarette-lighters
grease-proof paper bread postcards
a Coke at any time of day —

with their polite *thank-you*
and *how-are-you*

their concern for local matters the locals
have forgotten

foreign women busying themselves
rather too much some have said
in her hearing

but she loves what they achieve —

ought to be a saint's day for them
discovering

what they are capable of simply
by leaving as men have always done

by steeling themselves
they brighten unpromising street corners
with bold display-racks

of frightening two-day-old newspapers
The Guardian The News of the World
The Times

too late for her
taking up the weight of her bag

HIS SON SITS ALONE IN THE *BAR PROMO*

there is constancy
there is repetition
as if scrolling in the slant sun

they pass in flip-flops bikini bottoms
t-shirts
bruised with the clinging of black sand

certain of nothing
once he wakes thirsty each morning
except to ask what must hold —

whether this brooding mood of reassurance
that such a thing as love
even if unexpressed

remains till the moon's extinguished
how women love him to dally with this

try to soften
break themselves on him then turn aside

believing the failure
to be their own fault —

or is it as water he laps into their
secret places thrillingly
refreshingly

they shiver at his coldness

he chatters with the energy of birds
tiny waves beneath the bow of a tethered boat
slapping

slopping
women lift trembling hands to their heads
bare their teeth

one after another

HE CONSIDERS THE USES OF HIS MOUTH

sits down with one of those great writers
who managed to survive
nearer the Arctic Circle

who kept a scorpion under a glass
till he saw it visibly sickening

would fetch soft fruit
for it to sting

poison expelled it would be well again —

what has accumulated within him
over the years
he sees as incoherence now

as a submerged and unmapped ocean bed
invisible from the quayside

and the looked-for cure
to bring it into relation with language

though not mere eloquence this time
rather a purpose

more worthy than the need to persuade
than this blind
preservation of the healthy organism —

what must be loosened in his mouth
he thinks of these days
as some finer sense as stark contradiction

to his old occlusion
what must be loosened and laid open

to the multitude of things
laid open around him

more smile than sting

HIS SON HAS A VISION OF THE LAVA FLOWS

after ten years
then ten more lost at sea
his son would sometimes catch him fretting

at the school's new green security gate

watching each year-group
growing restive
fumbling with how to fulfil themselves

children
ignorant of how to work themselves
into their own lives —

like the island's native rock
blackened and pocked as a fossil sponge

completely unworkable
so the art of sculpture never took root
where tarmac ribbons

cut across fields of lava
razor-edges murderous to shoe leather —

still boys free-wheel off the road
at any hour of the day

to stand cooling
in the empty mouths of airless tunnels
no taller than themselves

where lava-flows boiled
each burrowing far beneath hardening crust

threads glowing huge and slug-like
undeflected heads down

single-mindedly
shouldering their way to the sea

HIS WIFE REMEMBERS THE HIGH CENTRE

in the Crater Zone
curves like highways giant magma slicks
the cone's last eruption

earth's seismic sneezing

black peppercorns the size of footballs
the shape of human heads

the size of black refuse sacks
big as overturned cars —

the last thing old men remember
that there were years before this darkness

this turning inside-out

these older oxidised rust-red levels
that begin to wrap themselves

in pine and stonecrop
the age for which all subsequent ages
pay unwilling price —

yet what she saw was more like eternity
grown short-lived
and what she witnessed

everything getting ready to dissolve
where old men cry out
watch that mountain watch that mountain

the bravado
of youngsters sneering shrugging up
fuck this shaking my fucking feet

her understanding how this must be
and that she can lay claim to neither

having waited too long

HE CONSIDERS WHAT THE YOUNG HAVE TO TEACH

to stand up invisible
as a forked child squalls in the whip
and withdrawal of waves

black sand thrown at shins and toes
sensing
the slither of ground beneath

and surely love this thrill of it
knifing him ecstatic

establishing its open wound

its soul-shaping progress the young know
yet unaware of —

trying to re-learn this
in part the effort not to flinch

as the dog he trained when young
coursing wild goat and deer and hare

like its master
no quarry able to slip away —

yet when he returned
almost unrecognisably changed infested
with ticks

half-dead from twenty years of neglect
an old rug
lay in the agave shade

dog and master thumping in recognition

barely able to drag themselves together
each as unpalatable
no finer test

the unlovable other

HIS WIFE DRIVES HERSELF THERE AND BACK

only in the High Centre could the shaman
be uncovered
his reputation for re-building those

who ascend through the pine belts
women particularly
pick across the lava fields

put themselves in his hands
feeling disappointed or depressed

bring their clicked back
or cracked heart —

she brings a lump in her right breast
he will spirit
to the basalt from which it was born

in its place
locates a piece of red coral
thought to transpose itself to human flesh

at his whirling prayer
though it must continue to ache

like a pulled tooth
to the probing helplessness of her tongue —

winding from the brutal fields
she tries the descent
crossing the long shadows of pine trees

enlivened by the hope of lying
precious again slowly

under a husband's kiss that will be ready
to touch and test and find

her out again

HE CONSIDERS THE LONGEVITY OF LOVE

beside the plash of blue fountains
fronting the Paradise Hotel

the shade-end of Flamboyant Street
he glimpses

her unfashionable blonde
medium-cut not prison-razored or wrapped

not seen folded
to the clipped *déshabillé* younger girls
begin to favour these days —

her body thickened
more severe in the black business suit

but the long-swing of the left hand hers
pale strands
on the nape of the neck hers

hers that bold
address to the world's sunny littoral

to the sunlit corner
beyond the blue of tumbling water
where now he is able to own the hurt —

no finer test
nor anything less than what his old self
would put to the sword

no more than the heart's bloody rent
she made of him

the gaping wound surviving still
restless in its stony bed

man's glittering and impassive ocean
to woman's cold moon

HIS SON FINDS HIMSELF LOOKING AT THE MOON

obscured by the flashing *Bar Promo* sign
the crescent moon

the night they met

the boy then with no thought of light
only gravity
her beauty as it drew him

across the dull universe of Tuesday night
the Place of Our Sacred Lady —

her glance across the tables
full of milky
outspokenness the whites of her eyes

the glossy black reserve in her pupil
those pale perfect breasts
his goal

in the ease of which he would find time
to reflect
on the nature the allure of such goals —

until the following Sunday evening
when they have outstripped
a whole series of unremarkable love songs

once more he walks
far out beyond the marina lights

once more to wrestle
with whether it's the moon must envy
his agitation and immobility

or whether
it is he who must envy the moon's
serenity

and slow movement

HE FAILS TO GRASP GOOD ADVICE

what passes for gods have not finished
with him yet

says one in the bar
who had things gone better
should by rights have been forgotten —

when you think you are done
there is still further to go
with something across your shoulder

you are not sure is not a gun
because you find yourself

travelling among people
who know nothing of the sea

eat no salt
have not seen a ship's purple sails
nor the long oars that drive them —

they ask
what is this *something-something*
across your shoulder

suggesting you lay it down
lay it right here
that you perform what rituals you recall

then perhaps if things had gone better
had this love
this hurt even the bright wind's shifting

this dream this joy
at the glittering brink of sight
where the sea-rise sways

to bring in another
this next of catches
from the salt's sharp throat

III
Riders on the storm

CAN TORRAS
for D and K

All the poor cork trees
stripped up to their knees
every four or five years –
the silver curling pelts
stacked in long battlements
far along the coast road.
As we drive higher, twisting
up the wooded hillside,
their bruised shins flash past.
Down in the valley, widows
of Franco's ill-fated
north-eastern plantations
move in with their sons
in the comfortable suburbs.
Others perish at home:
jerry-built blocks renovated
one apartment at a time.
We talk of how it feels
to have reached maturity
with just the common run
of grief and disappointment
though we could name many
who have been troubled more.
At the summit, two dogs
barking at the car announce
home – its wind-chime tones
re-shuffling combinations
in response to problems
set them by the breeze.

SUPPLY

More through a faint vibration of the air
on our skin than by the ear,

we feel his arrival and hurry out –
leave the unfamiliar house for a darkness that

to our urban eyes is solid pitch,
nothing close, no middle, no sense of distance,

just a freezing rural December night
and whatever we can feel beneath our feet.

And there he is, rear wheels slipping in the mud
frictionless as any proper god –

come with the intent of supplying us
with food and drink through the winter solstice.

Rotund, in the spill of his van's light,
a pair of plump hands on hips, legs apart,

he stands there laughing at his predicament,
then punches away at the faint

signal on his phone but the place is too remote.
We offer to help him out –

begin to stumble to and fro in the lane,
in his rear-lights each like a crimson-faced clown –

trying gravel shovelled from the farm drive,
trying terracotta roof tiles

someone has tipped beside the bramble hedge.
We search for anything we might wedge

in the black slithering mess under his tyres,
straw, cardboard, logs, ironic prayers.

But the van still snarls like a tethered beast
and rocks to and fro like a helpless

child that fights the confines of its cradle . . .
Then he dismisses us with a smile.

He sends us back to light and warmth,
saying something like *it's what I'm here for.*

We shut the door, relieved, to be honest.
We leave him to the closing vice of frost

and next morning scarves of mist
replace the dark that with him have vanished.

Wheel ruts, gravel, red tiles broken:
we laugh in daylight – did this really happen?

Outside, there is so little evidence to show.
Inside, shelves overflow.

CALLING IN THE DARK

As their son I hope to be
solicitous to the last
as three generations sit
by a dark Victorian sash
in a city pub, gazing out:
Sunday lunchtime, peaceful.
Even London translates
into something beautiful
as buses idle at the lights
quivering with spring rain.
Yet for the eldest two
the hours and minutes run:
the journey home is long,
both liable to fall,
he grows deaf, she finds it
exhausting to travel.
So I insist they call me,
if anything goes wrong.
Carefully, with her thumb,
she presses my number on
to her new mobile phone.
How many more such times?
On each occasion now,
the word is *'bye, goodbye.*

My phone shakes with her.
I pick it up and hear them
(hers buried in her bag,
keys pressed at random)
and for a while I listen
to her irritable tone
as she repeats words for him,
certain they're alone.

Now his anxious cry:
Look gal! It's here! Here!
It's painful to listen,
knowing they cannot hear
my voice muffled under
keys, compact, tissue paper,
my calling in the dark,
no more use than prayer.
Enough. I end the call.
I cannot bear to pry
on what is coming closer
and will carry them away.

EMERGENCY SERVICES

With our little ones, we like to show them
the speeding hulks of the emergency services.

Only yesterday, the red blast of a fire-engine
throwing its light like a trim blue weight.

Moments earlier, you gathered up your girl
and dashed to the curb for the black windows

of two white vehicles speeding to A & E.
The howl of squad cars becoming hypnotic . . .

And till now I never wondered what it might
be they learn. You say it's our concern

for one another: how we share the world.
Or perhaps we teach them cowed obedience,

pulling in as they pass. Or maybe it's no more
than aesthetics, bright lights, caricature.

RIDERS ON THE STORM

With no schedule to drive us,
we wait for rain to stop beside Ullswater's

southern lip, for the landlord of *The White Lion*
to determine when it's time to open.

Ducking through the door, Helen, Clive, Steve,
each a few weeks shy of university,

and I'm there too, heart awash
with absence, her love letters at looked-for drops,

the girl I feel leaving gradually
as the tedious route past Thirlmere to Catstye.

But it's OK for a while – passing midday snug
in a deserted pub

while outside the downpour gurgles, begins to blur
and double with the torrential roar

of the juke-box: The Doors the only thing
we key in, its electric piano's limpid fingering

like the give and tender recoil of water,
the lugubrious voice . . . Fifteen years later,

at his paint-spattered Père-Lachaise stone,
I remember that wretched lunchtime

under the wettest rain in England,
when I was too ill-formed to understand.

I barely displaced a drop of local weather,
could only conceive of myself as either

a body slumped beside a dry stone wall
or drenched and raging on the dramatic fell

on the path to Ambleside bus station,
its oily tarmac smoking under black rain,

her blonde voice fluent on the phone:
'You hear me?' I could not even hear my own.

SCRAPS
for Thomas

All I can stomach of cathedrals
these days is the detail.
Not the stand-back-and-gawp
that grows too rich for me –
the wide-angle too much,
the whole too vertiginous to please.

A cherub's backside is good to see.
His little pigeon-winged shoulders
fine for me – to be truthful
exactly the kind of thing
worth getting up to closely
if I'm on church ground at all.

Or arches. Or terracotta tiles.
Or the dusty glimmer of brass.
No more than a looker-on,
I walk with my six-year-old son,
confidently thinking I'm done
with the absence of faith

although something remains –
a single thread slipped the shears
passing on from me to him
becomes clear as we push
through the door's polished grain
slap-bang into the blurt

of ring-tone scraps, the street's
flagrant whine, its rapid fade
and sudden brake-light, the smash
and grab of shop-wisdom . . .

As one – as the touched horns
of a snail – we shrink in.

So this is what I hope for him:
a stronger belief than I knew,
that the solitary man
in his quietude need not
be scorned and ridiculed,
need not have plagued so bitterly

my boyhood – the guts
to see whole cultures have anchored
high tide in retreat,
though others deride it
and more: the few details I managed
in the cathedral before.

A TRUCK CALLED 'PERSEVERANCE'

Only the lucky, finishing
late breakfasts, glimpse
gaily-painted liveries,
lines of trucks trailing
faded green tarpaulins
and habitable trailers
like mid-century Pullmans
with their white roofs
and white window frames.
A thrill's already gone
round the playgrounds
as a '45 Scammell's
six-digit plates precede
polished maroon, yellow trim,
hubs, exhausts, grilles.
Unhitched, chocked – steel
bars are casually dropped
to ring cut-short clanks
around Priory Park . . .
A union flag is raised.
In rows, glossy frontages
propped and cross-braced,
A-framed, pyramidal.
Chassis-boxes swing open –
old sea-wood deployed
as rough props. A flat-bed
Ford sports a rampant
golden pony on its roof.
A late-coming truck
is called 'Perseverance'.
And so few personnel
accentuate this life
of objects: these working

drills of metal strut,
wooden pole, a thousand
wordless givens obeyed
and leather cash pouches
for a while locked away.
Browned with sweat and sun,
scattered torsos lug
brushed metal plates,
assemble the dull jigsaw
of the dodgem floor.
From park benches, the less-
than-lucky see it grow
like a circular nest,
like a rash in the grass,
progressively cloaking
its own dynamic . . .
In a Hawaiian shirt,
a tall man walks as if
it hurts to move at all.
See – depth and structure
under the falling sun,
striped roundabout tops.
See – conical bastions,
Octopus legs, the tilting
arms of Dive Bombers
like catapults readied
in distant squares.
See a camp, compact town,
an imperative flag-waving
all-too-likely city
that flaunts its allure
like a little Troy
you live in hope of,
you must lay siege to,
though ten years is nothing
to this working life.

TENBY CHURCH AQUARIUM

I
A water-filled vessel at the door.
We dip our fingers in the cold
and find a chilly, salty blessing.
Quickly try to shake it off
at the mock rock-pool edge –
its few jellies and crustaceans
squat and scary as gargoyles.

II
Now a gothic, nail-studded door,
draped with blue-sheened plastic,
slit to vertical ribbons that
clack-clack as we push past
into an old quarantine of hymns.
In naive unison they'd sing,
filling this place with thin water.

III
Bright rectangles on all sides
more like technicolour screens,
showing not the fisher of men,
rather the fish themselves
(the salty, the brackish, the fresh).
Their undeniable presence
surrounds our churchy whispering.

IV
In the darkness, children climb
onto the rails to be astonished.
Chewing at crusts, they shape
their questions, ask who it was
and how and why did they silence
and expel the old singing
for these lovely, lovely fish?

PETRARCH'S HEAD
died 1374

We can't shake this need to know your face.
Strong as love, we smash the peace
of Arqua with industrial cranes. We raise
the marble slab that glows pink as rose
that marks the place your body was laid,
that has long protected your remains,
the sticks, the plates, the skull, of course.
Then we find somebody's been here before.

Perhaps Fra Martinelli can explain?
His seventeenth-century ghost, let's raise
him fat as life and lucky to be whole.
Let's clear the fog of alcohol
that steeped his irreligious bones
and ask if it was greed that pricked him on

to smash his way into your tomb?
Is it Martinelli we must imagine climb,
kneel and thrust his hand into the filthy dark
to pull out – what? – an ivory stick,
a sheaf of mismatched ribby curves?
Though you'd lain there three hundred years,
did he filch your skull and run –
a thief lifting a loaf from a stone-cold oven?

If he did, how could Professor Canestrini
disturb you in the nineteenth century?
No common thief – though a loner again –
he abused you not with appetite but brains.
His motive for cracking open your tomb:
the art of poetry and perhaps a little fame.

In Canestrini's notebook we read
how 'in trembling hands' he held your head
and with his sense of the theatrical,
how sudden pressure on your 'impractical
poet's skull' crushed it to dust!
Nothing withstands a professor's touch!

Or is this a lie? Now it's empirical men
we trust: Vito Terribile Marin
from Padua – a scientist– our contemporary
who re-built the face of St Anthony.
Yet even Marin has been taken aback
by the bizarre but indisputable fact:
the skull his white-coated assistants took
from under the rose-pink marble block,

from a pile of proven masculine bones,
was not yours. It was a woman's . . .
Petrarch's head – a mystery no longer.
Surely the answer lies with beautiful Laura,
the girl like an idea you glimpsed one day –
Laura, who took your breath away,
greedy thief and snatched your heart as well,
allowing nothing of herself at all.

Laura, your world! Written to untruth:
you said she died first. It must have been you.
How else could she manage to give head
for a broken heart? She understood
too late, seeing you laid to rest,
hurt by what she had failed to express.
Only then were your words able to pierce her,
persuade perfect flesh to shed a tear,

convince her the uncreative must sing
a breathless committed new heart into being –
at last your work moved her to requite
her head in your tomb for yours when she died:
the poet's head happy in love's dark place
and love's tongue relieved in his embrace.

KEATS

A building site apparently,
though we all resist,
prefer the pastoral
of nightingale and musk rose

as he lay upstairs,
listening to Brown banging
the servant-girl by the door,
her little repeated cries.

And the one star sank
in the adjoining house.
Her sigh, odour, distance
each a reason why

the hoops of suffering
must bring us to ourselves.
Or perhaps a premonition:
the boat's keel cutting

the Neapolitan harbour,
too sick to wonder,
but listening constantly –
the sounds of this house.

A hammer and a nail.
Shouts of workmen busy
with the elevation of wealth.
And still he listens

leant now on a pillow,
the clock's iambic *tick-
tock* ahead of him still,
limping perfectly along.

ONE THING AFTER ANOTHER
for Anna

The ivory, angular vertebra I found
the day after the day my daughter found

and tried out her new word – *fuck* –
was bony, spiky to touch, rough as fuck.

I thought: *Depths! Essence! Bone!*
She bent to it, touched it, turning bone.

Leave it, I called. She said, *Is it real?*
White in the grass the contrast was real.

CALDEY LIGHTHOUSE

I

One more holy island,
this called cold, though it's not.
We come to it past ice-cream stalls
that have broadened their appeal
with scuba gear and spades,
six pounds the round trip.

II

We board by walking on water
over a stilted causeway,
swaying six feet above meagre surf.
We hang in the salty air,
feel like souls on judgement day,
cannot shake out of our heads
the euphoria of ozone
or the idea that our fate
is no longer in our own hands.

III

A buckaroo ride across waves:
salt lips, children squealing
round the elbow of the bay
with my blue-shirted arm
thick as a sailor's rope behind them.
They lean back and howl
as bright water is beaten from the prow
to come gasping back at us
again and again till we
do not notice the green bulk
risen from the pelting blue.

IV

Disembark to the lush quiet
of a carless space. Peacocks
walk like extravagant spirits.
Still we go on, unguided,
through latch-gates, up thistle lanes
to the tall white bodying forth
on the island's highest point.
Here, warm summer nights
come and go; the lamp's sweep
uncovers sleek rocks and seals.
But this afternoon,
it appears little more than bone,
end on in the earth:
socket and head and shaft.

V

Last night, we watched moths
catch the far-off gleam –
the reflection of bone-light
(the distance to be travelled).

As they leap, their wings drop
a smattering of flight dust
across leaves on the balcony.
We say *sleepy-dust* to the children.

VI

It's hard. At chorus-time,
naked, kneeling at the open window,
curtains splayed to the mist.
Oak, ash, elm – their heads up
like separate planets,

distant stars, transmitting
the dry sounds of birdsong.
They loom and fade off
like the curly heads of parents,
impassive faces vanishing
down the edge of night,
bright water beaten from the prow.
I lean back and howl.

WILDERNESS

1.

Resoundingly, against
the wooden dock,
the little slippings
of the latest canoe
stay beneath my feet
for hours on dry land
as fish after tawny-finned
fish betray themselves
to our hook and worm,
to the arid debate
about whatever species
of freshwater bass
they might prove to be.
Above our temporary
bed, hand-painted fish
travel left and right
as if they would leave
a vacuum in the frame –
but here the sleeping
is heavy and up-close
as if we ruled king
and queen of the lake,
the lake a fertile
Nile, its flood plain
the cumulative sense
of well-being that is
the right and proper end
of all questioning.
In their crowds, trees
move restless at night,
their sighing easy,
their no need to fret.

2.

See my flesh and blood
here, bright and true
as a sun on the rise,
she launches herself
from the anchored platform,
flies into the air
over the blue-lit water,
unaware of tethers
beneath the surface,
of ropes, trailing weed,
slime, mud and scales
stiffening in reaction
to her vigorous action.
Here she is, hanging,
all parts my daughter,
curling like a ball,
the sudden black water,
while the white trunks
of ten thousand trees
cram the lake shore
and enclose her round.
All sounds hang back
as she arcs and peaks,
begins her slow bow
to the pull of gravity,
the smash of water,
the great churning
of foam and white limbs
yellowing as they spread
to carve out stroke
after buoyant stroke
into the swims of joy
and grief she'll tread.

3.

Stammering in the wind
where it comes dawdling
round the promontory,
a fiery tethered flight
at the fourth attempt
from the darkest wood
on the opposite shore.
Not far below, angles
of the lake fling out
black insights that
in a moment transmute
to blue and white mirrors.
The bird is climbing
up the blockish line
of trees – no further.
She cannot make it.
Not today. Not this way.
Although a child gamely
tugs the slack string,
the maths conduct
to negative equations:
all buoyancy lost,
black wings, red fire
in danger of drowning
though no more than
twenty feet from shore.
After a few moments
wrestling with the lake,
her father staggers
to dry land – already
shaking drops of water
from the firebird,
a mercury flickering –
happy to play midwife
to this sodden birth.

4.
She catches my eye,
the fore-square address
as she stands reciting
our order to be sure,
but can then no longer
hide when she limps
towards the kitchen door.
Her sweet young face,
she keeps it focused
on the dull job despite
the thinness of limbs
that leads every table
to stare at the hunch
of her back – brings
a shiver of sympathy
at how she lays herself
aside for our sake.
Or is the face a mask?
What we take as real
a well-rehearsed drill?
What if this pricking
of remote love, pity,
seeing her ugly body,
is mistaken? What if
she walks home tonight,
opens the screen-door
to one more able,
more capable of seeing
past crookedness
to the heart's process,
its every stoop, start,
the soul's particular
strength, shapeliness,
in its right place?

5.
This must be the limit
of our day's journey,
the northern-most point
on the lake of bays
since we have driven
this pontoon boat
through overcast hours,
little peepings of sun,
to the water's exchange
of white, grey, blue,
black, green to be here,
moored at this creaking
dock as if to wait.
This, how it will seem
at the end of the day,
after the great storm
that will have turned
the lake-top white
in its swerving north –
it will surround us
with a billion tiny
falling drops, each one
a momentary concave
flowering of the lake,
of fresh rain falling
into fresh water.
We will wait this out
so that – already warm,
our jackets cast off,
slow screws groaning
to the final berth –
we will be raked by
the last of sunlight,
each of us undampened
in praise of the day.

6.

The surface of the lake
has its pleasures too.
Some days it seems
to say look up always
whether the prospect
is blue or grey or else
strike inwards, within,
it appears to cry
although you struggle,
even though the murk
seems unfathomable,
a thing of gleams
and flashes, clock-slow
movement or the rapid
approach of danger,
of escape, of nothing
that is clear at all.
More than anything
it is this apparent
flickering to no purpose,
to fill a given space
that appears so apt,
it seems so beautiful
it leads us to hope
that it might allow us
no reason to flinch,
nor bully, nor brawl
but shift in the wind,
with the flood: try not
to hold on but let go.

7.
The hardest of lessons
and for how many years
have I been devoted
to its cause – studied
what is apparently
only a losing game,
the effort to move on
only a little deflected,
only always changed.
Begin by abandoning
sandals, summer clothes,
maps and rods, charms,
old chairs, even books –
a corner folded down
where we left off reading
in the drifting boat.
Now photographs found
slowly to be missing.
Now files corrupting,
their loss the start
of another remembering,
nothing utterly lost
if we have once closed
with them as this canoe
nosing a wooden dock
fights the slip, slide,
the troublesome waves
and the wind's buffet
till its gentle bass
booms securely home
in this delicate love
that allows the world
to wear us, a brooch,
allows us our wearing
of this wilderness.